Ways into Science

Seasons

Peter Riley

W
FRANKLIN WATTS
LONDON • SYDNEY

Franklin Watts
Published in Great Britain in 2016
by The Watts Publishing Group

Copyright images © Franklin Watts 2014
Copyright text © Peter Riley 2014
(Text has previously appeared in Ways into Science:
Seasons (2003) but has been comprehensively
re-written for this edition.)

Editor: Julia Bird
Designer: Basement 68

PB ISBN: 978 1 4451 3481 9
Library eBook ISBN: 978 1 4451 3843 5
Dewey classification number: 620.1

Printed in China

Franklin Watts
An imprint of
Hachette Children's Group
Part of The Watts Publishing Group
Carmelite House
50 Victoria Embankment
London EC4Y 0DZ

An Hachette UK Company
www.hachette.co.uk
www.franklinwatts.co.uk

FSC
www.fsc.org
MIX
Paper from
responsible sources
FSC® C104740

Photo acknowledgements:
All photos Roy Moller except: Bildagentur Zooo/
Shutterstock: 26t Blend Images/Shutterstock: 8b. Jacek
Chabraszewski/Shutterstock: 9t. Dainis Derics/Dreamstime:
18t. ER_09/Shutterstock: 13b. Ewa Studio/Shutterstock: 5bl,
26b. Geothea/Shutterstock: 17b. Dmitri Gordon/Shutterstock:
17c, 28b. Jaroslaw Grudzinski/Shutterstock: 13t. Gvision/
Dreamstime: front cover tl. Dave Head/Shutterstock: 5tr, 14.
H Helene/Shutterstock: 24b. Mihail Ivanovic/Dreamstime:
25cr. Iakov Kalinin/Shutterstock: 13c. R Kasius/Dreamstime:
front cover cr. Maxim Khytra/Shutterstock: 4, 12b.Viktoriya
Kirillova/Dreamstime: 18b. Lilkar/Dreamstime: front cover bl.
S & D & K Maslowski/FLPA: 6c, 6b, 7t, 7c. Bruce Macqueen/
Dreamstime: 5br, 19. Dmitry Maslov/Dreamstime: 24t Wayne
Mckown/Dreamstime: 15t. Nejron Photo/Shutterstock: 12t.
Pitchi/Dreamstime: front cover br. Platslee/Shutterstock: 16b.
Paul Reeves Photography/Shutterstock: 17t. Wendy Rentz/
Shutterstock: 5cr, 16t. Rck953/Dreamstime: 21. Theowl84/
Dreamstime: 20. Aaron West/Dreamstime: 25. E J White/
Shutterstock: 15b. Tracey Whiteside/Shutterstock: 3, 8c.
Elena Zajchikova/Shutterstock: 27t & c.

Contents

Four seasons

In many parts of the world, there are four seasons.

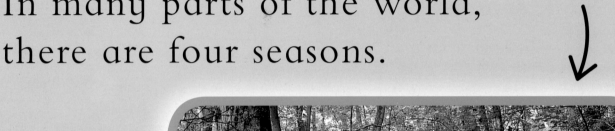
Spring

Summer

autumn

winter

Leabharlanna Poiblí Chathair Baile Átha Cliath
Dublin City Public Libraries

Look outside. Which
season is it now?

7

Rain or shine?

In every season, the weather can change from day to day.

There are cloudy and wet days all year round, but there are usually fewer of them in summer.

There can be sunny days at any time of year. A sunny day in winter is cold, but in summer it is hot.

It can be windy any time,
but the wind blows stronger
in autumn or spring.

We usually
only get snow
in winter or
early spring.

What is the weather
like today?

Weather record

Harry records the weather in each season. For ten days in January, April, July and October he does four things.

1. Checks if the sky is clear or cloudy. (You must never look directly at the Sun.)

2. Finds out how warm it is with a thermometer.

3. Measures the rain with a rain gauge.

4. Finds the wind type using this table.

What is seen?	Type of wind
Nothing moving	No wind, calm
Leaves rustle	Light breeze
Flags fly	Gentle breeze
Small branches wave	Moderate breeze
Large branches sway	Strong breeze
Whole trees sway	Gale

Record the weather in different seasons. What does your table look like?

The Sun and seasons

In daytime, the Sun moves
across the sky in a curve.
It rises at dawn. It gets higher
in the sky until midday.

The Sun sinks in the afternoon.
It sets in the evening.

In winter the Sun's curve is low and short. It does not shine for long. This makes the weather cold.

In spring the curve is higher and longer. The Sun shines for longer. This makes the weather warmer.

In summer the curve is at its highest and longest. The Sun shines for the longest time. This makes the weather hot.

What do you think the Sun's curve is like in the autumn?

Spring

As winter changes to spring, the days get longer and the weather is warmer. It rains a lot.

Plants start to grow.

Some new animal life also begins in spring.

Birds make nests and lay eggs.

What do you think happens to the eggs? Turn the page to find out.

Summer

Bird eggs hatch in spring and summer.

At first, the parents feed their chicks. Over time, the parents teach the chicks to feed themselves.

The chicks grow up and leave the nest.

Other young animals, such as foxes, are also taught to find food.

Many plants have flowers in summer. Insects visit them for nectar. They carry pollen between the flowers.

pollen

What happens to flowers when insects bring them pollen? Turn the page to find out.

Autumn

Many flowers grow into fruits. The fruits are ripe in summer and autumn.

The fruits contain seeds, which will make new plants in the spring.

In autumn, some animals get ready for winter.

Squirrels gather nuts to eat during the long winter.

What does a bat do in the autumn? Turn the page to find out.

19

Ready for winter

Bats find a safe place to sleep. They sleep through the winter. We say they hibernate.

This bat will wake up in the spring when there are more insects flying around and food is easier to find.

In autumn some birds join up in big flocks

They fly away to a warmer place for the winter.

In spring they return again. This is called migration.

How can you help birds that stay for the winter? Turn the page to find out.

Winter

In the winter birds sometimes cannot find enough food to eat.

Sophie is putting out food for them.

Can you find a place to feed birds in the winter?

Many plants need lots of warmth and light to grow properly. In the cold, dark winter they stop growing.

Seeds, bulbs and roots lie deep in the soil, protected from cold weather. They grow shoots again as the winter ends.

What happens to plants next? Turn the page to find out.

Plants through the year

In spring and summer the extra heat and light make plants grow.

Plants grow leaves and flowers.

In autumn flowers and leaves die back and the fruits become ripe. Some fruits form parachutes and blow away.

Some plants do not die back in autumn. Some of them have woody stems covered in bark.

The bark keeps out the winter cold.

What kind of plants have stems like this? Turn the page to find out.

Trees through the year

Trees have stems like this. Some trees have leaves all year round.

The holly has spiky leaves. It has red berries in the autumn and winter.

The pine has long, thin leaves like needles. It has cones that hold its seeds.

Some trees lose their leaves each year. In autumn this tree's leaves turn orange and start to fall off.

By the winter, all the leaves have fallen off.

What are the trees like where you live? What season is it?

Useful words

Breeze – a type of wind that has different strengths.

Bulb – a ball made by the stem and leaves of some plants.

Fruit – the part of a plant that holds the seeds.

Gale – a very strong wind.

Hibernate – to sleep through the winter.

Migration – the journey made by an animal to travel from a cold place to a warm one.

Nectar – a sugary liquid made by flowers. Insects use it as food.

Pollen – a powder made by flowers. It spreads to other flowers and makes them grow fruits and seeds.

Rain gauge – something that collects rainwater and has a scale on it so you can measure the depth of the water.

Ripe – fruits that are fully grown.

Season – a time of the year that has a certain kind of weather such as hot and dry in summer and cold and snowy in winter.

Seed – a part of a plant that grows after the flower has got some pollen. It grows into a new plant.

Thermometer – something that measures how hot or cold it is. We call this the temperature and measure it in degrees.

Some answers

Here are some answers to the questions we have asked in this book. Don't worry if you had some different answers to ours: you may be right too. Talk through your answers with other people and see if you can explain why they are right.

Page 7 This will depend on the time of year and place. Not all places have four seasons. Some places have a wet and a dry season.

Page 9 This will depend on the season. Try to describe as many things about the weather as you can, such as is it sunny, cloudy, windy, still, raining, fine, snowing, hot or cold.

Page 11 You could make a table with these headings – day, sky, temperature, rain, wind. You may like to just tick the table when it is raining and measure the amount of water in the rain gauge at the end of ten days.

Page 13 The Sun's curve is lower and shorter than the one in summer. It is like the Sun's curve in spring.

Page 27 This will depend on the place and the season. Describe the leaves on other trees - are they bursting out of buds, fully grown, turning brown or have they fallen to the ground?

Index

About this book

Ways into Science is designed to encourage children to think about their everyday world in a scientific way and to make investigations to test their ideas. There are five lines of enquiry that scientists make in investigations. These are grouping and classifying, observing over time, making a fair test, searching for patterns and researching using secondary sources.

• When children open this book they are already making one line of enquiry – researching seasons. As they read through the book they are invited to make other lines of enquiry and to develop skills in scientific investigation.

• On page 7 they are invited to try out their observational skills.

• On pages 9 and 27 they are challenged to try out their observational skills and record in detail.

• On page 11 they are asked to make observations over time, including taking measurements and gathering data. Later they can use all the data to look for a pattern.

• On page 13 they are asked to make a prediction based on the information they have read.

• On pages 15, 17, 19, 21, 23 and 25 they are asked to make predictions based on their general knowledge.